When I Grow Up...
Doctor

Written by Clare Hibbert

Illustrated by Mike Byrne

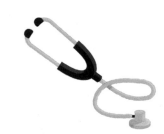

Consultant: Dr Vashti Mason

LADYBIRD BOOKS

UK | USA | Canada | Ireland | Australia
India | New Zealand | South Africa

Ladybird Books is part of the Penguin Random House group of companies
whose addresses can be found at global.penguinrandomhouse.com.

ladybird.com

First published 2015
001

Printed in China

A CIP catalogue record for this book is available from the British Library

ISBN: 978–0–723–29469–6

Contents

What do doctors do?

Being a doctor is a very important job. Doctors help people who are sick. They also treat diseases and help us to stay healthy.

Seeing patients at the surgery

GPs are local doctors. They treat everyday illnesses. If a patient has a serious disease or problem, the GP sends him or her to the hospital.

Seeing patients in their homes

Sometimes patients are too poorly to visit their GP. The doctor talks with them on the telephone or visits them in their home.

Seeing patients at the hospital

Hospital doctors treat emergencies and serious health problems. Lots of doctors work in hospitals.

The doctor's surgery

People who are ill or need medicines visit their GP at the surgery. Some surgeries have just one GP and others have several.

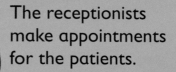

The receptionists make appointments for the patients.

The patients tell a receptionist when they arrive, or use a self-service check-in machine. Then they wait in the waiting room to be seen.

The doctors have their own rooms where they see their patients. They call the patients in from the waiting room, one at a time.

Daily life

At the surgery, the GP sees as many as thirty or forty patients every day. Each appointment lasts about ten minutes.

The doctor asks the patient questions to work out what is wrong. Once she knows, she might give the patient a prescription for medicine that will help him get better.

The doctor takes the patient's temperature with a thermometer to make sure it's not too high.

The doctor looks into the patient's ears with an otoscope. Sticky ears are a sign of an ear infection.

The doctor looks into the patient's eyes with an ophthalmoscope to see if they are healthy.

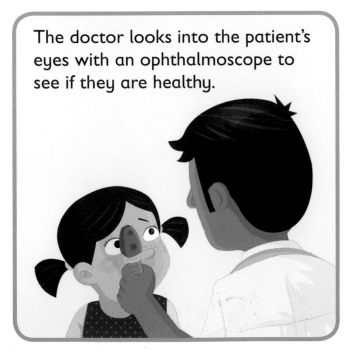

The doctor uses a stethoscope to listen to the patient's lungs and heart to hear if they are working properly.

Doctor's kit

The doctor uses all sorts of different tools, machines and other equipment. These things help the doctor to do his or her job.

Computer

The doctor can look at a patient's notes on the computer for details about past illnesses.

Examining table

The doctor's room has a special bed in the corner where patients can lie down to be examined.

Scales for weighing patients

The doctor may weigh a patient to check that she is a healthy weight for her age.

Throat stick and latex gloves

The doctor puts on latex gloves and uses a throat stick to press down the patient's tongue and view his throat.

Bandages for protecting wounds

The doctor has many different bandages and dressings. He uses them to protect the patient's wounds.

Blood pressure monitor

The doctor puts a special armband on the patient. It is pumped with air to check the patient's blood pressure.

Nurses

Nurses are a big help to doctors. They work in surgeries, clinics and hospitals. Some visit patients in their homes.

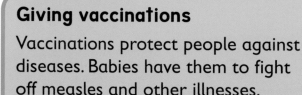

Giving vaccinations

Vaccinations protect people against diseases. Babies have them to fight off measles and other illnesses.

Testing for asthma

Nurses ask patients to blow into a machine called a spirometer to work out if they have asthma.

Taking out stitches

Stitches help a wound heal neatly. Some must be removed by a nurse. Others dissolve on their own.

Changing a dressing

Bandages hold dressings in place while wounds heal. The nurse puts on new bandages every couple of days.

Taking blood

Nurses take blood samples from patients. These are tested to find out about the patient's health.

Cleaning ears

Ear irrigation gets rid of wax that can block a patient's ears. The irrigator is filled with warm water.

The human body

Doctors need to know all about the body and how it works. When they study, they learn the names and jobs of every body part.

Brain
The brain is the body's control centre. It is protected by the skull.

Lungs
The lungs take in oxygen from the air. They pass it into the heart, where it can enter the blood.

Heart
The heart pumps blood around the body. It beats about 70 times a minute.

Liver
The liver cleans the blood by removing harmful toxins.

Stomach
The stomach
breaks down food.
It is part of the
digestive system.

Muscles
Stretchy muscles
make the body move.
They are fixed to all
the bones.

Bones
The body has a
framework of bones
called the skeleton.
Bones can regrow
if they break.

Hospital specialists

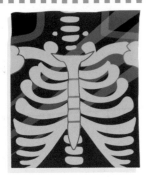

Some hospital doctors are experts in one kind of disease or part of the body. They are called specialists. All their patients have similar needs.

Paediatrician

This doctor helps babies and children. Children's bodies are different from adults' bodies. Paediatricians specialize in their health.

Orthopaedic surgeon

This doctor is a bone expert. He uses X-rays to look inside the body and see the bones. He treats broken bones and bone diseases.

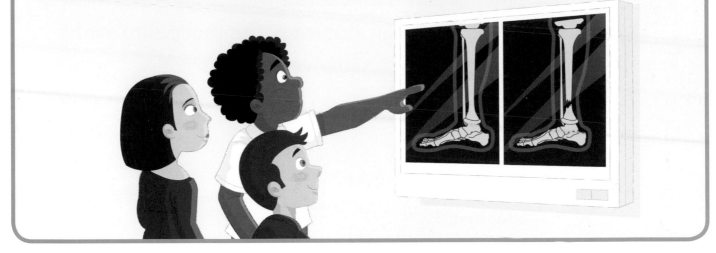

Ear, nose and throat specialist

This doctor treats patients who have diseases that affect their ears, nose or throat. She uses an endoscope, which is a tube with a video camera attached to it, to see inside the nose.

The maternity ward

The part of the hospital that looks after new mums and their babies is the maternity ward. It has doctors, midwives and nurses.

Ultrasound scan

Pregnant women have check-ups at the hospital. The sonographer scans their tummy to show a picture of the baby growing inside.

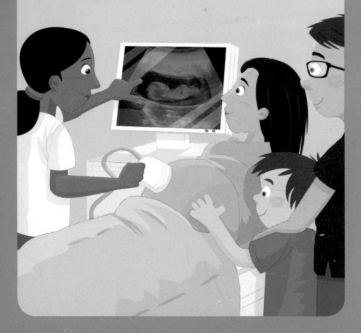

Giving birth

Some women have their babies at home, but most go to hospital. The midwife is there to help.

Specialist baby care

Some babies need extra care. They might have been born too early or had a difficult birth. They stay in hospital for a few weeks so the doctors and nurses can give them special attention.

Doctors on call

Most hospital doctors have to spend some time 'on call'. This means they are not working, but if there is an emergency they must go in.

Getting the call

The doctor carries a bleeper when he is on call. It makes a noise if the hospital needs him.

At the hospital

The hospital has called the doctor to the hospital. A patient is being brought in by ambulance.

Arrival by ambulance

Paramedics wheel in the patient on a stretcher. He is rushed to the emergency room.

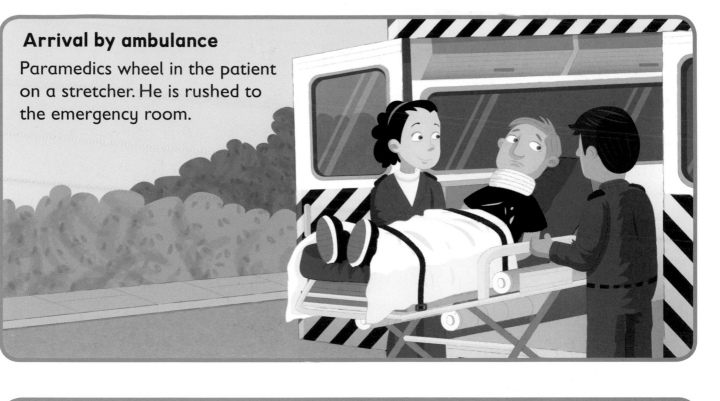

Looking after the patient

The doctor examines the patient and settles him into the ward to be cared for.

The operating theatre

The operating theatre is where patients have operations. The doctors who carry out operations are called surgeons.

Scrubs

Everyone in the operating theatre wears clothes called scrubs – green or blue tops and trousers. They wear a clean, new set for each operation.

Masks and gloves

Everyone in theatre wears gloves and masks. This is so no germs reach the patient.

In theatre

Before the surgeon operates, the anaesthetist gives the patient medicine to put him to sleep.

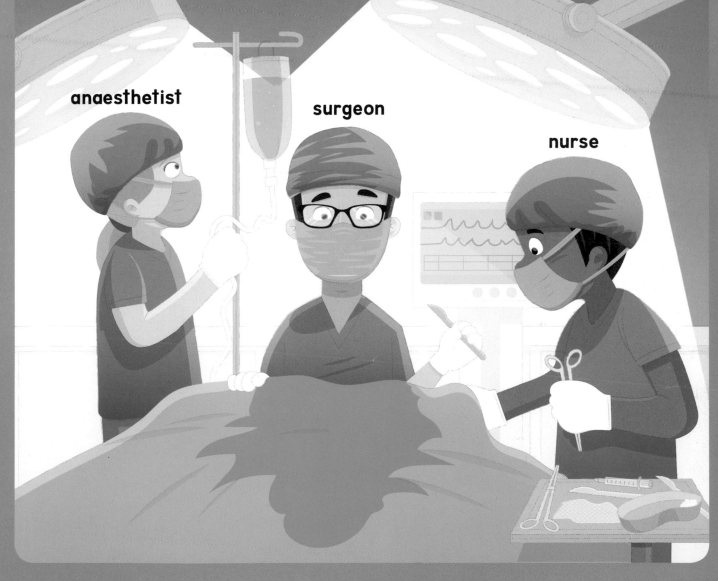

anaesthetist

surgeon

nurse

Working together

Many people work at a hospital, taking care of patients. They include cleaners and porters, nurses, paramedics and pharmacists.

Pharmacist

The hospital has its own pharmacy, where medicines are kept and given out. The pharmacist is in charge of the medicines. The doctor gives the patients a prescription to take to the pharmacist.

Hospital porter

Hospital porters move patients around the hospital if they can't walk. They use wheelchairs and beds with wheels.

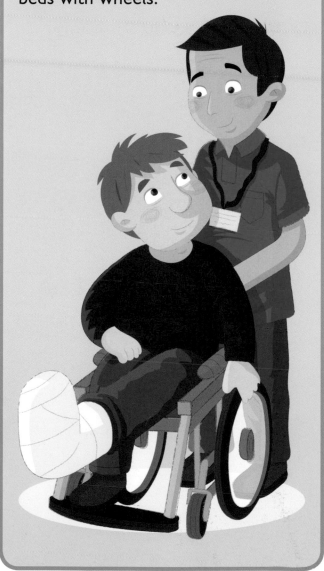

Triage nurse

This nurse talks to patients when they arrive in an emergency. He passes the notes to the right doctor who will then treat the patient.

Around the world

All over the world, people need doctors to look after them. Some places do not have enough doctors or medicine.

Vaccinations

Children can be protected from certain diseases with vaccinations. These doctors and nurses are injecting babies and children with a vaccination so they will be safe from a dangerous disease called polio in the future.

Helping in disasters

After an earthquake or other disaster, a country might need extra doctors to treat all the injured people. Emergency doctors also treat people hurt in fighting or wars. Armies around the world have their own doctors and nurses.

Through the ages

The history of medicine stretches back a long, long time. Even cave people had ways of treating people who were ill!

Transporting the patient

In the past, sick people were moved around on horse-drawn carts or carriages. Just over 100 years ago, ambulances with motor engines were introduced.

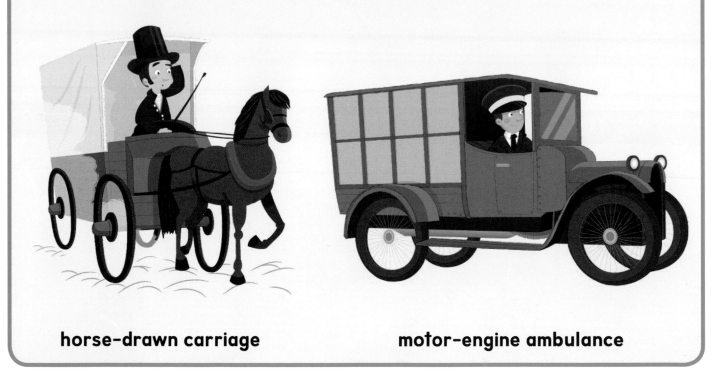

horse-drawn carriage   **motor-engine ambulance**

Mending broken bones

In prehistoric times, people used clay to set broken bones. The ancient Egyptians wrapped pieces of tree bark next to broken bones to keep them straight as they mended.

using clay

using tree bark

Examining the body

Long ago, doctors had to use just their own ears to listen to their patients' chests. A French doctor invented the stethoscope around 200 years ago. Listening through the wooden tube made sounds louder.

listening by ear

using a wooden tube

Being a good doctor

Becoming a doctor takes a lot of work. There are new things to learn about all the time, but helping people in need makes it all worthwhile.

Student doctors learn how to treat patients with all kinds of illnesses. They watch how trained doctors work to prepare themselves.

Doctors need to ask patients the right questions and listen to their replies. They must be able to recognize the signs of different illnesses.

Doctors should be kind and caring. When a patient is scared or worried, a good doctor will reassure them that they will be well looked after.

Doctors look after us at every stage of our lives, from the moment we are born. Thanks to their work, people live longer and more healthily than ever before.

Glossary

anaesthetist   A doctor who is trained to give a patient a special medicine before they have an operation. The medicine puts the patient to sleep and stops them from feeling any pain.

examine   To look at very carefully.

GP   Short for 'general practitioner'. The name for a doctor who treats everyday illnesses.

latex   Very fine rubber used for doctors' gloves. The latex is thin enough for doctors to feel through, but no germs can pass through it from the doctor to the patient or from the patient to the doctor.

operating theatre   The place in a hospital where surgeons perform operations.

paramedic   An ambulance worker trained to give emergency first aid as a patient is rushed to hospital.

pharmacist   Someone who is trained to give out medicines.

prescription   A note from a doctor saying what medicines a patient must take.

specialist   A doctor with expert knowledge in a particular subject, such as heart disease.

toxins   Something poisonous which is made inside the body. The liver removes toxins from the blood.